Shaggy
SHIH TZUS

SMALL BUT STURDY!

LIVELY! ALERT! PROUD!

ABDO
Publishing Company

Anders Hanson

Consulting Editor, Diane Craig, M.A./Reading Specialist

Published by ABDO Publishing Company
8000 West 78th Street, Edina, Minnesota 55439.

Copyright © 2009 by Abdo Consulting Group, Inc.
International copyrights reserved in all countries.

No part of this book may be reproduced in any form
without written permission from the publisher.
Super SandCastle™ is a trademark and logo of
ABDO Publishing Company.

Printed in the United States.

Editor: Pam Price
Content Developer: Nancy Tuminelly
Cover and Interior Design and Production:
   Anders Hanson, Mighty Media
Illustrations: Bob Doucet
Photo Credits: Shutterstock

Library of Congress Cataloging-in-Publication Data

Hanson, Anders, 1980-
   Shaggy shih tzus / Anders Hanson ; illustrator Bob Doucet.
     p. cm. -- (Dog daze)
   ISBN 978-1-60453-619-5
   1. Shih tzu--Juvenile literature. I. Title.

SF429.S64H36 2009
636.76--dc22
                       2008037965

Super SandCastle™ books are created by a team of
professional educators, reading specialists, and content
developers around five essential components—phonemic
awareness, phonics, vocabulary, text comprehension, and
fluency—to assist young readers as they develop reading
skills and strategies and increase their general
knowledge. All books are written, reviewed, and leveled
for guided reading, early reading intervention, and
Accelerated Reader® programs for use in shared, guided,
and independent reading and writing activities to support
a balanced approach to literacy instruction.

CONTENTS

The
SHIH TZU

Shih tzus are small, **energetic** dogs. They are smart and friendly. Shih tzus have round heads with short, hairy **snouts**. Their coats are long and shaggy.

Shih tzus are one of the oldest **breeds** of dogs. They are originally from China. *Shih tzu* means "lion dog" in Chinese.

FACIAL FEATURES

Head

Shih tzus have round heads. Their **snouts** are short and hairy.

Teeth and Mouth

Shih tzus have small, sharp teeth.

Eyes

Shih tzus have large, round eyes. They are usually dark.

Ears

Shih tzus have long, droopy ears.

BODY BASICS

Size

Shih tzus can grow up to 11 inches (28 cm) tall. They usually weigh 9 to 16 pounds (4 to 7 kg).

Build

Shih tzus are solid and sturdy. Their bodies are a little longer than they are tall.

Tail

Shih tzus have long fur on their tails. Their tails often curl over their backs.

Legs and Feet

Shih tzus have short, straight legs. Their feet are round and well padded.

COAT & COLOR

Shih Tzu Fur

The shih tzu has a thick coat of long fur. Underneath the long fur is another layer of short, **woolly** fur. Shih tzu fur can be white, gray, gold, red, or black. Most shih tzu coats have two or more of those colors.

WHITE FUR

GRAY FUR

BANDED COAT

RED WITH BLACK TIPS

GOLD WITH BLACK MASK

Shih tzus come in many different colors and coats.
The photos here show just a few examples.

GOLD FUR

RED FUR

BLACK FUR

LIVER COAT

SOLID WHITE

SOLID BLACK

HEALTH & CARE

Life Span

Most shih tzus live to be 10 to 15 years old. Some healthy shih tzus live up to 18 years.

Grooming

Shih tzus should be brushed often to prevent tangles. Their fur should be cut regularly.

Shih tzus shed very little. They may be suitable for people with **allergies**.

VET'S CHECKLIST

- Have your shih tzu spayed or neutered.
- Visit a vet for regular checkups.
- Ask your vet which foods are right for your shih tzu.
- Clean your shih tzu's teeth and ears once a week.
- Avoid exposing your shih tzu to very hot temperatures.
- Brush your shih tzu often.

EXERCISE & TRAINING

Activity Level

Shih tzus like to go on short walks. But they mostly like to be lazy with people indoors. Their short legs are not suited for lengthy exercise.

Obedience

Shih tzus can often be independent and **stubborn**. They need consistent training. Training should focus on rewards instead of punishments.

A Few Things You'll Need

A **leash** lets your shih tzu know that you are the boss. With a leash, you can guide your dog where you want it to go. Most cities require that dogs be on leashes when they are outside.

A **collar** is a strap that goes around your shih tzu's neck. You can attach a leash to the collar to take your dog on walks. You should also attach an **identification tag** with your home address. If your dog ever gets lost, people will know where it lives.

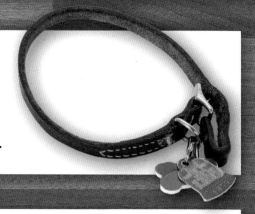

Toys keep your shih tzu healthy and happy. Shih tzus like to chase and chew on them.

A **dog bed** will help your pet feel safe and comfortable at night.

ATTITUDE & INTELLIGENCE

Personality

Shih tzus are friendly and loving lapdogs. They need lots of attention.

Shih tzus are very brave. They make good watchdogs. They bark loudly if they are startled.

Intellect

Shih tzus are not very smart dogs. A new command may need to be repeated about 80 times before the dog learns it!

12

All About Me

Hi! My name is Sally. I'm a shih tzu. I just wanted to let you know a few things about me. I made some lists below of things I like and dislike. Check them out!

Things I Like

- Being treated like a princess
- Sitting on people's laps
- Playing fetch
- Having my coat brushed often
- Going for short walks
- Hanging out inside

Things I Dislike

- Being ignored
- Going on long, fast runs
- Being left outside all day
- Feeling really hot

LITTERS & PUPPIES

Litter Size

Female shih tzus usually give birth to three or four puppies.

Diet

Newborn pups drink their mother's milk. They can begin to eat soft puppy food when they are about four weeks old.

Growth

Shih tzu puppies should stay with their mothers until they are eight weeks old. They grow until they are about two years old.

BUYING A SHIH TZU

Choosing a Breeder

It's best to buy a puppy from a **breeder**, not a pet store. When you visit a dog breeder, ask to see the mother and father of the puppies. Make sure the parents are healthy, friendly, and well behaved.

Picking a Puppy

Choose a puppy that isn't too **aggressive** or too shy. If you crouch down, some of the puppies may want to play with you. One of them might be the right one for you!

Is It the Right Dog for You?

Buying a dog is a big decision. You'll want to make sure your new pet suits your lifestyle.

Get out a piece of paper. Draw a line down the middle.

Read the statements listed here. Each time you agree with a statement from the left column, make a mark on the left side of your paper. When you agree with a statement from the right column, make a mark on the right side of your paper.

I think pampering a dog is fun.	☐	☐	I want my dog to entertain itself.
I want to be adored by my pet.	☐	☐	I want an independent pet that gives me space.
I like to take my pet lots of places.	☐	☐	I prefer to leave my dog at home.
I spend a lot of time at home.	☐	☐	I'm not home very often.
I love to brush fur.	☐	☐	I think brushing fur is boring.
I think short noses are cute.	☐	☐	I'm grossed out by snoring, snorting, and snuffling sounds.
I like to go for short, easy walks.	☐	☐	I love to go biking, running, and swimming.
I don't like hot weather.	☐	☐	I love the heat.

If you made more marks on the left side than on the right side, a shih tzu may be the right dog for you! If you made more marks on the right side of your paper, you might want to consider another breed.

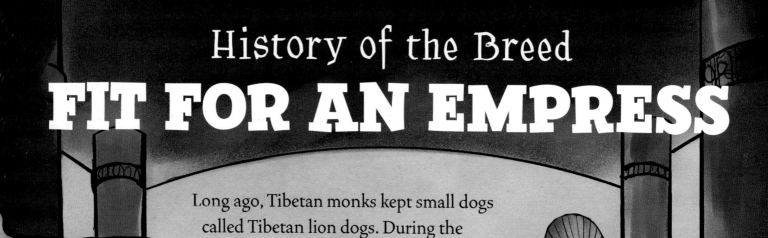

History of the Breed
FIT FOR AN EMPRESS

Long ago, Tibetan monks kept small dogs called Tibetan lion dogs. During the 1600s, the monks sent some of these dogs to Chinese emperors as gifts.

Legend has it that the small Tibetan dogs became a favorite of Empress Tzu Hsi. Her servants **bred** the Tibetan lion dogs with other small dogs she kept. This produced the dog we know today as the shih tzu.

19

Tails of Lore
THE LION DOG

Shih tzu means "lion dog." It is said that more than 1,000 years ago, when **Buddha** was traveling the **countryside**, a shih tzu always went with him.

If anyone threatened **Buddha**, the shih tzu would turn into a lion! Then Buddha would climb onto the creature's back and ride away to safety.

FIND THE SHIH TZU

A   B   C   D

Answers: **A)** Chinese crested **B)** miniature pinscher **C)** Yorkshire terrier **D)** shih tzu (correct)

THE SHIH TZU QUIZ

1. Shih tzus have short, hairy snouts. **True or false?**

2. Shih tzus have short legs. **True or false?**

3. Shih tzu fur should be brushed often to prevent tangles. **True or false?**

4. Very hot temperatures are good for your shih tzu. **True or false?**

5. Shih tzus are never stubborn. **True or false?**

6. You should buy your shih tzu puppy from a breeder instead of a pet store. **True or false?**

Answers: 1) true 2) true 3) true 4) false 5) false 6) true

GLOSSARY

aggressive – likely to attack or confront.

allergy – a body's negative response to a particular substance.

breed – 1) a group of animals or plants with common ancestors. 2) to raise animals, such as dogs or cats, that have certain traits. A *breeder* is someone whose job is to breed animals or plants.

Buddha – the founder of Buddhism. Buddha is also called Siddārtha Gautama.

countryside – land in a rural area.

energetic – showing great activity.

snout – the projecting nose or jaws of an animal's head.

stubborn – difficult to manage or handle.

woolly – resembling wool in appearance.

About SUPER SANDCASTLE™

Bigger Books for Emerging Readers
Grades K–4

Created for library, classroom, and at-home use, Super SandCastle™ books support and engage young readers as they develop and build literacy skills and will increase their general knowledge about the world around them. Super SandCastle™ books are part of SandCastle™, the leading preK–3 imprint for emerging and beginning readers. Super SandCastle™ features a larger trim size for more reading fun.

Let Us Know

Super SandCastle™ would like to hear your stories about reading this book. What was your favorite page? Was there something hard that you needed help with? Share the ups and downs of learning to read. We want to hear from you! Send us an e-mail.

sandcastle@abdopublishing.com

Contact us for a complete list of SandCastle,™ Super SandCastle,™ and other nonfiction and fiction titles from ABDO Publishing Company.

www.abdopublishing.com • 8000 West 78th Street
Edina, MN 55439 • 800-800-1312 • 952-831-1632 fax